First published in Great Britain 1984 by Colour Library Books Ltd.
© 1984 Illustrations and text: Colour Library Books Ltd.,
   Guildford, Surrey, England.
Color separations and text filmsetting by Llovet S.A., Barcelona, Spain.
Printed and bound in Barcelona, Spain by Rieusset and Eurobinder.
All rights reserved.
Published 1984 by Crescent Books, distributed by Crown Publishers, Inc.
Printed in Spain
ISBN 0 517 451476
h g f e d c b a

PRINCE HARRY
and the Royal Family

Trevor Hall

CRESCENT BOOKS
NEW YORK

They sang *Land of Hope and Glory* more lustily than usual on the last night of the 1984 Proms. Of the balloons that rose and wafted above the Albert Hall's traditionally exuberant audience, there was a noticeable predominance of blue. A home-made banner bearing the message 'Well Done Di' was draped over one of the maroon and cream balcony boxes. It seemed superfluous that James Loughran should, towards the end of the conductor's customary farewell speech to the Promenaders, announce that 'our Princess of Wales has given birth to a son,' but when he called for three cheers, they were given spontaneously and to the echo of that vast auditorium.

It was Saturday 15th September, and those cheers were themselves echoes of a whole series of joyful public reactions to the news that, six hours earlier, Diana Princess of Wales – the most instantly popular royal celebrity of the century – had given birth to her second child. The first members of the general public to know were the 500-strong crowd which had gathered outside the now celebrated Lindo Wing of St Mary's Hospital, Paddington ever since the announcement that the royal mother-to-be had arrived there with Prince Charles at 7.30 that morning. For her, as for her loyal – or merely curious – admirers, the wait was by no means as long as it had been at the time of Prince William's birth. True to form, the second child arrived with greater ease and speed than the first – nine hours from his mother's entry into hospital, as opposed to the 16 hours it took for Prince William to be delivered – and Prince Charles spoke with obvious relief when he told well-wishers that evening, 'The delivery couldn't have been better. It was much quicker than last time.'

Perhaps that was just as well. For all their patience and tenacity, the growing crowds sensed in that dampish September air an uneasy similarity with that June day in 1982 which, despite being the first day of summer, could afford only a mixture of cool breezes and drizzle. But any second thoughts about playing the waiting game to the bitter end were briskly brought into line by the periodic comings and goings at the hospital door – most of them quite unconnected with the royal birth itself, but each heralded by the sporadic activity of almost a hundred press and television personnel. Ever hopeful of capturing just the right picture, ever wary of missing the shot that might prove vital, they hoisted cameras to faces with the split-second simultaneous timing of a regiment shouldering arms. Perched atop ladders – some so old and battered that they might have seen the Queen Mother married; others, spanking new aluminium jobs which looked to have been hastily purchased for this occasion alone – the newsmen had possibly the most uncomfortable wait of all. Perhaps one day the Palace will concede that some of them might after all deserve the occasional medal.

Even for them, however, the news of the royal Prince's birth was delayed for an hour while Prince Charles, who had been present at the birth and had heard his second son's first whimpers, telephoned his parents at Balmoral. The Queen was said to be delighted – as indeed were all the other members of the Royal Family. Princess Anne was notified while she was helping her husband, Captain Mark Phillips, to run the horse trials which for the second year in succession were being held in the grounds of their home, Gatcombe Park. Princess Margaret heard the news while in Glasgow for a charity engagement and she was, in her own words, 'absolutely delighted.' The Spencer family were also quickly informed. 'Wonderful news,' said Lady Sarah McCorquodale, Princess Diana's elder sister, while her second sister, Lady Jane Fellowes added, 'We are very happy for them all.' Predictably it was Lord Spencer himself – proudly showing visitors around his stately home at Althorp when he received the news – who enthused longest and loudest. His main thoughts were for Prince William who, he thought, would be 'really thrilled. It will be lovely for Prince William to have a little companion, a playmate. Nice to have someone to fight with. And I'll tell you this,' he added firmly, even a little aggressively, 'I hope he will one day play cricket for Gloucestershire.' Prince Charles clearly had other ideas. Carefully dodging all public enquiries about a third child, he seemed to commit himself with the mischievous observation, 'We've nearly got a full polo team now.'

Much of the activity which surrounds a royal birth is these days predictable – from the intense and sometimes jittery police presence around the hospital to the champagne-popping revelries in front of Buckingham Palace as the official bulletin is chained to the railings, or mounted on a gilded easel for all to see. But in one respect at least, this birth broke a tradition. Ever since the Queen's marriage in 1947, every royal mother –

the Queen, Princess Margaret, the Duchess of Kent, Princess Alexandra, the Duchess of Gloucester, Princess Anne and Princess Michael of Kent – have given birth first to a boy, then to a girl. We are gradually becoming accustomed to Princess Diana being just that little bit different, so perhaps it was no surprise – even though many were a touch disappointed – that a son, rather than a daughter, was the result of her second pregnancy. That has not happened in British royal history since the Duchess of Gloucester (now Princess Alice) gave birth to boys at her only two confinements, in 1941 and 1944.

And it is from the Gloucester family that Prince Charles and his wife chose Henry as their new baby's first name. Just as the choice, in 1982, of William reflected the memory of Prince William of Gloucester, who had died in an air crash ten years earlier, so Henry finds a precedent as the name of that ill-fated Prince's father, the late Duke of Gloucester, who also died ten years before his latest namesake, outliving King George V's five other children. Like the old Duke himself – a sound, dutiful, if rather unimaginative man – the name Henry has an outmoded ring about it, and the news that the Prince and Princess had chosen it for their son did not please everyone. Nor did the familiar version, Harry, at first. One critic thought it worthy only of a regular at the local pub, though most, somewhat reluctantly, agreed that it did have the common touch which other royal names conspicuously lacked. Henry's ready identification with those budding young Mayfair aristocrats – the good-time 'Hooray Henrys' – might also have contributed to the initial surprise, and certainly explains why the name never featured among the front-runners with the bookmakers, as did George, Philip, James, and even Simon.

But Henry, as few schoolchildren ever forget, has been the name of eight of Britain's kings, though fortunately, perhaps, the characters and careers of those monarchs offer no consistent guide to the reasons why the name should have been chosen in 1984. Henry I proved a successful statesman within his own kingdom; Henry II, despite his reputation as the murderer of Thomas à Becket, began a strong expansionist campaign abroad. Henry III's most applauded achievement is the rebuilding of most of Westminster Abbey, while Henry IV's short reign left him a broken man – a 'sinful wretch,' in the words of his own last will and testament. Henry

V lives as the Shakespearean hero, the victor of Agincourt; Henry VI as the saintly, murdered martyr whose reign in heaven was presumably more glorious than his storm-tossed rule on earth. To Henry VII is credited the establishment of a strong Tudor dynasty, a united Crown and the firm beginnings of our naval traditions, while his son Henry VIII has won over as many admirers by his undoubted charm and ebullience as he has alienated by the Machiavellian methods which prompted Charles Dickens to describe him as 'a blot of blood and grease upon the history of England.' So, even discounting those childless Henrys who were the sons of James I, Charles I and George II, the new Prince's name has, to say the least, equivocal connections. Perhaps that is why his parents have decided that he will be known as Prince Harry. It softens the inevitable historical edge, and acknowledges public temptation to abbreviate and familiarise forenames which may otherwise sound rather old for their owners.

All of Prince Harry's other three names – the Prince and Princess of Wales again followed the tradition set by the Queen of allotting four Christian names to each child – have much more recent royal connections. Charles requires no justification; not only is it the name of the baby's father, but also of his uncle, Viscount Althorp, younger brother of Princess Diana. Likewise Albert, which was the first name of Earl Spencer's father, and was obligatory for all royal males during Queen Victoria's day. It was she who, writing to her son about the names for the future King George V, insisted that 'all dearest Papa's *male* descendants should bear *that* name, to mark *our line* just as I wish all the girls to have Victoria after theirs. I lay great stress on this,' she added imperiously, 'and it is done in a great many families.' David, which was the last of Edward VIII's seven Christian names, and the one by which he was known within his family, is believed to have been chosen for Prince Harry in memory of Sir David Bowes-Lyon, the Queen Mother's favourite brother and constant childhood companion, who died in November 1961, only five months after Princess Diana was born. Princess Margaret will have been particularly touched by the choice of Prince Harry's subsidiary names, all of which are those she chose – also in November 1961 – for her son Viscount Linley. And the Principality of Wales will feel especially proud that the name David recalls their patron saint, while Henry celebrates the great Welsh

Tudor family which governed Britain for almost a century and a quarter.

As if to prove how easy it is to dispense with some dyed-in-the-wool royal practices, Prince Charles and Princess Diana decided not to wait very long before announcing Prince Harry's names. The names of all four of the Queen's children were not made public for at least a month after their respective births – a tradition which Prince Charles discontinued in 1982 by announcing Prince William's names exactly a week after his birth. But that was only a stepping stone to the run of events after Prince Harry was born: it was barely nineteen hours later that his names were known. Furthermore, the announcement was made, not by any sort of formal proclamation, but by Prince Charles' genial Canadian Press Officer, Victor Chapman, who trotted out of the hospital just before noon on 16th September, and crossed the road to tell the waiting crowds of the proud parents' choice.

Mr. Chapman's announcement was only one brief highlight of that day. About two hours earlier, Prince William, spick and span in a crisp white shirt and cherry red shorts, had arrived with Prince Charles to visit his mother and take his first look at his new baby brother. He climbed the steepish steps of the entrance manfully, with purpose, and fortunately without incident, and when he came out again, accompanied by Barbara Barnes, the nanny he will now have to share, he gave the delighted onlookers a sudden, if somewhat floppy wave, which had them shrieking with surprise and rapture. Prince Charles stayed with his wife and baby son for another hour, leaving for lunch at Kensington Palace, and returning again to take Princess Diana home. And how, at last rewarded for all their patience, everyone cheered and clapped and shouted when the scarlet-clad Princess finally appeared, her baby completely unseen as he nestled in his warm, woollen coverings, fast asleep in her arms. With Prince Charles by her side, she stood for a few seconds, blushing profusely, doing her best to keep her shy, reluctant smile on her face, and just giving the occasional hint that she would really rather be inside the waiting car and away. Soon she was, and within twenty-two hours of seeing her off to hospital, the staff at Kensington Palace welcomed her back again. It was almost symbolic of the disruptive life which the Royal Family is sometimes obliged to lead, despite its identity as a close-knit family unit, that within less than an hour, Prince Charles was off to play polo at Windsor. A perfect end to a very successful personal season for him, he celebrated the events of the weekend by scoring three goals – though unfortunately he finished up on the losing side.

News of the safe and satisfactory outcome of the Princess' second pregnancy was like nectar to millions of her admirers who for two years had thirsted for positive confirmation of a widely held belief that she had wanted children in quantity and at speed. Thanks to the Princess herself, their hopes had been raised as early as November 1982 when, with almost indecent haste – it being only three months after Prince William's christening – she made a casual reference to the possibility that her son would soon be playing with brothers and sisters. The remark was bound to have immediate repercussions and, sure enough, on her next walkabout, she was asked whether she might be expecting again. Her reply –'You must be joking. I'm not a production line, you know' – was as instant as it was peppery, and served both to counter her previous suggestion of a nursery soon to be full of royal children, and to put down all further talk of increasing the size of her family. The aftermath of the anorexia scare and the preoccupying tours of Australia, New Zealand and Canada effectively discouraged public speculation on the subject. But it was in Canada itself that the prospect was raised again – this time courtesy of Prince Charles who, when opening the Festival of Youth in St John's, Newfoundland, talked of the responsibility 'we now have towards our child at present – and, I hope, several more in the future.' His wife immediately lowered her blushing features as the listening thousands began their mental interpretations of the significance of his reference. Then, only two days later, Newfoundland's Premier, Brian Peckford, spoke publicly of the conversation he had had with the Prince and Princess, and insisted that 'I got the distinct impression that both of them would like to have more children.

For all that they lacked detail, comments like these were quickly seized upon to confirm what by now everybody seemed to anticipate – that, with three major Commonwealth tours behind her, the Princess would soon be providing Prince William with a nursery companion. All seemed settled when, only a fortnight after beginning her holiday at Balmoral, she flew to London, tra-

velling under an alias, for a twenty-four hour stay which coincided with her gynaecologist's first day back at work after his own three-week vacation. Was it coincidence? Yes, said Buckingham Palace; the Princess had merely wanted to visit a member of her staff in St Thomas' Hospital. It was purely a private matter and, 'if she is having a baby, it will be announced at the proper time.' But a mere social visit did not seem to justify the expense and upheaval of a 900-mile return trip, and the carefully worded official explanation did nothing to stop what from then turned into a flood of curiosity. 'That's a very personal question,' retorted the Princess hotly to a woman who, the next day, asked her point-blank whether she was pregnant. But even that didn't work. Evading a definite answer is no substitute for giving one. 'She looks too well not to be pregnant,' said one onlooker on the same occasion. 'There was a special glow in her face,' affirmed another – and so it went on. National newspapers – starved, as tradition dictates, of real news during the silly season – took up the theme with such incessant enthusiasm that even Debrett's habitual aloofness from such a popularist pastime seemed momentarily compromised as its former editor speculated on the choice of names. The trumpeting of successive Press revelations gave one little girl the courage to walk up to the Princess during one of her official visits, put her hand on her tummy and ask how the baby was. 'Did I hear right?' asked the Princess, looking surprised and somewhat embarrassed. Fortune-tellers were not slow to pitch in with their contributions. The ebullient and irrepressible Russell Grant, almost scorning the blandness of anticipating nothing more than the next royal child, forecast that the Princess would have no fewer than five in all; while an American astrologer predicted that on this occasion she would have triplets. Two would be girls, the third a boy who would force the Queen to abdicate, usurp the throne from Prince William, and restore the Empire.

Amid such technicolor invention, Buckingham Palace did its best to restore a sense of balance. Victor Chapman reiterated that the stories had no foundation and that there was definitely no pregnancy. Lady Sarah McCorquodale, Diana's sister, said that she agreed with the Palace's sentiments that the rumours were mere speculation and rubbish. Gradually, these authoritative leads were followed. The producer of a Glasgow variety show, which the Prince and Princess

were to attend, decided to ban all baby jokes for fear of causing embarrassment, and one national newspaper almost adopted the policy of denial as its own personal crusade against the more outlandish fancies of its rivals. The cumulative effect of all this, however, eventually tipped the balance the other way. By the end of October, there was growing concern that the Princess was experiencing difficulty in conceiving – an anonymous 'close friend' described her as 'tense and tearful' – while the continental weekly *France Dimanche* attributed to her unchanging slim figure her ability to conceal her pregnancy by virtue of the anorexia she was still suffering! It took an end-of-year announcement that the Prince and Princess would be visiting Italy the following October to convince the world that there would be no prospect of a royal baby in 1984. The bait, if bait it was, was duly taken, and although the Princess continued to be the Press celebrity she has been for almost four years – Christmas at Windsor, New Year at Sandringham, a skiing holiday in Liechtenstein, and a brief official visit to Norway all provided good opportunities for photographs and stories – it was no longer due to the possibility of renewed motherhood. The conviction that she was not with child was accepted universally, if tacitly – although one medical journalist suggested as late as February that the Princess could be suffering from weight loss and stress, both of which were factors which could prevent conception.

That statement was made to look ridiculous when the Princess, cleverly choosing her moment, announced on 13th February that her second pregnancy had begun. Royal-watchers, those professional pundits who thrive on the hope of offering predictions which are not only right but also timely, were initially taken by complete surprise, though they quickly regained their composure to comfort themselves by a backward glance at Diana's sparkling eyes and broad smiles during her recent visit to Oslo. In those features, and in every other royal gesture or pose during that hectic weekend, they belatedly invented all the indications of the good news she was obviously bursting to disclose.

'I was so thrilled and delighted, I nearly fell off my dressing-table stool in my excitement.' The writer was Queen Mary; the date May 1941; and the news the impending birth of her fourth grandson, Prince William of Gloucester. The idea of Queen Mary falling off a chair in excitement –

or for any other reason – is almost as alien to those of common clay as, say, a vision of Queen Victoria taking a sauna or Prince Albert feeding coins into a fruit machine. Certainly, the official Court expressions of royal reactions to news of this kind have always been suitably restrained, almost to the point where, these days, any comment publicly made by royalty immediately becomes news. Following timeless Court practice, the Queen did not publicly make a personal statement about the prospect of her fourth grandchild, and was only *said* to be delighted, though guests at the following day's Investiture at Buckingham Palace found her in sparkling form. Prince Philip, rarely drawn into domestic conversation on such occasions, except perhaps for the purposes of wit and laughter, ventured the revelation that 'we are all very pleased' at a Windsor Rugby Club dinner that day. The Prince and Princess of Wales themselves were of course pleased with the news – again that was only reported by the Palace Press Office, who also confirmed that Diana was in excellent health. It was left – as often seems to be the case these days – to Princess Michael of Kent to volunteer something a little more colourful. She told a businessmen's lunch-time gathering in London the day after the announcement, that the Royal Family were 'ecstatic' over the news – though a subsequent toast fell flat when the wine waiters failed to serve up the champagne! The Princess of Wales' mother, Mrs. Shand Kydd, was even more forthcoming. 'I am excited.' she said. 'They're really happy days when they're safely in the world.' Her second daughter, Lady Jane Fellowes, echoed the family's mood. 'Lovely news', she called it. 'I am very pleased. It's smashing.'

Meanwhile, Buckingham Palace braced itself for the inevitable jamming of its switchboard with messages of congratulation and enquiry, and the flood of telegrams and gifts which invariably follows news of a royal pregnancy. Everyone seemed agreed that, after all the frustrated speculation, the Princess' timing was impeccable. Such a nice change, someone said, from the political manoeuvrings in the Kremlin after Andropov's funeral and from that tedious sensationalism on one of the oddest events that month – the marriage of Elton John. Only why, asked one loyal subject, didn't Diana announce the news a day later – the perfect winter pick-me-up on St Valentine's Day? No matter, the maternity wear trade, newly recovered in the wake of Prince William's early days, was wreathed in smiles, while the good wives of Coventry set to, knitting bootees, mittens and bonnets in readiness for the Princess' first official outing – a visit to the Jaguar car factory at Allesley – two days after the announcement.

It is well within human memory that royal pregnancies, once intimated only by the mysterious official announcement that a Princess had suddenly cancelled her forthcoming engagements, were hardly ever spoken of in public until doctors and midwives actually began to move into the Palace to supervise the confinement. The last war seemed to liberate matters a little, and the newspapers subsequently felt able to interpret the mystique of Palace jargon for the benefit of their readers. In this way, for instance, Prince Charles' conception in 1948 became public, if somewhat reverentially hushed, knowledge from the moment they announced that 'Princess Elizabeth will undertake no public engagements after the end of June.' It seemed a satisfactory ritual, this device to spare the Palace the embarrassment of acknowledging intimate personal truths, while allowing the public to form its own conclusions in its own, no doubt less dignified way. But it was exposed as a dusty and derisory anachronism when it was worked for the last time in 1959. The Queen's third pregnancy, suspected in June and known to the family by early July, was intended to be kept secret until after a six-week tour of Canada which she was due to complete with Prince Philip that month. That was an achievement in itself. In the first week of the visit, she began to suffer from morning sickness and it was consequently not long before the Press in Canada began to notice, and its British counterparts began to question. Then, as the Queen was obliged to thin out her engagements to cope with her indispositions, the speculation really began. Despite what was regarded as disrespectful guess-work in the French-speaking Quebec papers that a baby was on the way, it seems scarcely to have occurred to the British that the Queen might, after a nine year gap, be expecting again, and the rumour was therefore confined to purely medical surmise – sinus trouble again, exhaustion, diet – even collywobbles. Eventually, a week after her return to Britain, the announcement was made. It said no more than that the Queen would be cancelling all future engagements, and in the light of what went before, this thinly veiled secrecy sounded positively ridiculous. So when, less than two years later, the time came for Princess Margaret

to disclose her first pregnancy, it was officially announced, in so many words, that she was indeed 'expecting her first child.' The Duchess of Kent followed the same formula in 1961, and Princess Alexandra in 1963. By that time, even the Queen's fourth pregnancy – she was expecting Prince Edward in September 1963 – was disclosed in sensible and straightforward language.

Reluctantly drawn into admitting the obvious, the Royal Family's next obstacle to liberation during pregnancy became the traditional cocooning of its mothers-to-be. Official engagements were, until the 1970s, all but taboo well before there was any risk of things becoming evident. Somehow, it just did not do to see royalty with child in public, perhaps owing to a fear of voyeurism in addition to an undoubted element of personal self-conciousness or even distaste. Shortly before Prince Edward's birth in 1964, for instance, the Queen refused to allow her Christmas message to be televised, and, on her subsequent – strictly private – travels to and from Sandringham, she was wrapped in a huge fur coat which conveniently concealed her condition while at the same time keeping her warm. It was Princess Anne who broke the mould when her son Peter was expected in Silver Jubilee year. Already well known – indeed almost notorious – for never shirking her duty to say what had to be said, she had no qualms now about doing what had already been planned. That meant carrying out as many arranged engagements as her condition would allow. She was in full public view throughout the summer of 1977, and there was something refreshing, not to say characteristically blunt about the sight of her tramping the course at numerous horse trials that Autumn, wearing voluminous donkey jackets or huge sweaters well and truly stretched over her.

Few people thus harboured any doubts about Princess Diana's attitude to impending motherhood in the public eye, and both her pregnancies have been famous as much for her natural, unstuffy, almost overtly proud approach as for anything else. What did take her admirers – and possibly her few detractors – by surprise was her willingness to go one better than all her royal relatives and actually talk frankly on the subject with whoever cared to bring the matter into the conversation. As a result, her walkabouts have become even more popular and eminently reportable, spiced as they have been with the latest tittle-tattle straight from the horse's mouth. As with her first pregnancy, the Princess lost no time in coming forward with details of her second. On that very first visit to Coventry, she was already regretting the prospect of losing her figure – and how everyone, remembering those superb slinky evening dresses and her stylish, figure-hugging casuals, sympathised with her! They sympathised even more when, after six weeks, she confessed she simply couldn't throw off the old bug-bear of morning sickness which had plagued her so persistently when she was carrying Prince William. 'I haven't felt very well since Day One,' she confided to a housewife in Leicester at the end of March. 'I don't think I am made for the production line.' But she soon cheered up. 'It's all worth it in the end,' she added. By early June she had steeled herself against the temptations of her celebrated sweet tooth, and was refusing gifts of butterscotch during a visit to a sweet factory in Wales. It was part of a vigorous fitness campaign which included regular exercise and frequent dips into the swimming pool at Highgrove. At the end of June, she was proudly telling well-wishers that she had swum thirty lengths the previous weekend. And, as if to emphasise her positive thinking, she added that she was hoping for a girl this time.

Prince Charles was also hoping for a girl, though when the explanation for his choice turned out to be the need for somebody to look after him in his old age, he set every feminist in the land against him. One of them hoped that he wouldn't leave it too long 'before making preparations to ensure that caring for him is more of a joy than a burden' and that he would not single out one daughter alone for such a potentially risky job. It was a valid point to make. One has, after all, only to look at the rather sad fates of the dutiful Princess Beatrice and Princess Victoria of Wales, whose enforced devotion to widowed mothers – Queen Victoria and Queen Alexandra respectively – restricted their outlook and activities, and frustrated any ambitions they may have had. But perhaps such thoughts take Prince Charles' possibly jocular remark too seriously, for there was no doubt that, whatever parenthood had done to him, it had not deprived him of his sense of humour. He roared with laughter when, having congratulated the Jaguar car workers on the efficiency of their production line, they congratulated *him* on *his*, and he no doubt sat back in amusement as the rumours gained

ground that his wife was expecting twins – a myth which he chose not to nail until July.

Indeed, over the seven months between the announcement of the expected birth and the event itself – a much quieter spell, incidentally, than the corresponding period before Prince William was born – no issue created as much public speculation as the much-hailed possibility that royal twins were on the way. Though a rarity in Prince Charles' genealogy, twins are most recently found in two branches of the Queen Mother's family. Her nephew, the 16th Earl of Strathmore, who died in 1972, had a twin sister Nancy, who predeceased him, dying at the age of only 41 in 1959; while the four children of the Queen Mother's brother Michael included twin daughters, of whom one, Lady Mary Colman, became godmother to none other than Princess Diana herself, at her christening at Sandringham in 1961. In the Princess' own family, the incidence of twins in recent generations is much more frequent. On her father's side, her aunt, Lady Anne Wake-Walker is the mother of twins, as is her maternal aunt, Mary, elder sister of Mrs. Shand Kydd. The fourth Baron Fermoy, Diana's grandfather, was also one of twins, while his widow Ruth can boast a father who was himself a twin. These facts made the bookmakers fairly cautious when Diana first announced her news, and they offered odds of only 25-1 against twins. But one firm suddenly stopped taking bets on this possibility one day early in April, after punters had tried to place up to £650 simultaneously at each of four separate London branches. It was just about the time when the Princess' first ultra-scan was reckoned to have been administered, and the bookmakers had their suspicions about the *bona fides* of their customers. 'They weren't exactly wearing coronets or ermine robes, but they seemed to be people who could have a little knowledge from the inside,' a spokesman said. The expectation of twins was strengthened in June and July after anonymous reports that Harrods had been delivering two cots to Kensington Palace, and that Diana herself had been spotted buying everything from baby towels to shawls in pairs!

Both Prince Charles and his wife will have been pleasantly surprised, not just by the comparatively quiet time they have experienced waiting for their second child, but in particular by the absence of unpleasantness. The early days of Diana's first pregnancy were marred by some unforgiveable acts of Press intrusion, including the now infamous Eleuthera incident, when photographers snapped her, bikini-clad, on a private beach where, in her fifth month of pregnancy she was attempting to enjoy a brief holiday. By the time of Prince William's birth, she had also had her fill of ill-informed talk which included accusations that she was out of sympathy with the rest of the Royal Family, and that she had all but come to blows with the Queen on the question of where her child was to be born, and how it should be brought up. This time, everybody seemed much more relaxed about the whole affair. Even the more sensationally-minded corners of Fleet Street lost the heart to stir up false dramas when, for instance, she left half way through a performance at the Royal Opera House in June because of the intolerable heat, or was absent from subsequent Buckingham Palace garden parties, or the Braemar gathering, or, worse still, suffered the shock and sadness of her favourite uncle's suicide in mid-August. Perhaps the feeling of *déjà-vu* contributed to the more measured reporting of the Princess' progress second time around, but it is more likely that the indisputable increase in her maturity and her proven ability to cope under the most intense personal pressure were factors which would make nonsense of a repeat of the sort of trivial stories which had circulated so widely in 1982.

Of course it was natural that, of the two children, Prince William's coming should provoke the longest and loudest orchestration. The visible strengthening of the direct line of succession has always carried its own special fascination for the British, and occasions which have extended that line have always been focuses for anticipation and, ultimately, celebration. For all that, it is a sobering thought that, of the 54 immediate successors to the Throne since Alfred the Great, only thirteen have been the firstborn of their immediate predecessors, while 25 have been younger brothers – or sisters, whether older or younger – of sovereigns or their successors. In some measure, those statistics owe something to the times when kings fell regular victim to the ambition of dynastic or territorial rivals – the days when, according to Shakespeare in his *Richard II*,

Some have been deposed, some slain in
war,
Some haunted by the ghosts they have
deposed,
Some poisoned by their wives; some
sleeping killed,
All murdered...

But even in the more stable political and constitutional atmosphere since, for instance, the accession of George I in 1714, only five out of ten monarchs succeeded as firstborn heirs, while the last hundred years alone offer two striking examples of how the burden of sovereignty was destined for the second child, but remained concealed for decades behind the hopes and aspirations popularly attributed to his senior, until death or abdication removed that elder man from the scene. So it is no idle pursuit to envisage circumstances in which this latest addition to the Wales family might justifiably be heralded and welcomed with as much public interest and intensity as was Prince William. One has only to remember how comparatively quietly the Queen herself came into the world to realise that the awesome trappings of monarchy and a thousand years of royal history sometimes await the most unlikely candidates.

For all that, the odds must favour that the new baby, like his uncles Prince Andrew and Prince Edward, will be able to grow up in relative privacy, and therefore comparatively normally. It has always been the aim of Prince Charles and his wife to achieve this degree of normality for their children – on the basis that they should delay as long as possible the day when their innocence is tarnished by the final realisation, with the same perplexity and even horror which Prince Charles himself experienced, of who they are and what they must do. On the whole, the Prince and Princess of Wales' policy of 'little and often' has succeeded. In the two years since his christening, for instance, Prince William has been the subject of four photocalls in his own right – one in New Zealand, one to celebrate his second birthday, and two in the run-up to successive Christmases. They have been spaced out to alternate with a couple of official photographic sessions – one at Christmas 1982, the other shortly before his journey to Australia the following Spring – and his various holiday trips to and from Scotland have not been too difficult for the Press to photograph. Sometimes this is even done with his parents' undoubted cooperation: his mother encouraged him to wave for the benefit of photographers when they returned to London after 1983's summer holiday at Balmoral, while Prince Charles pointedly allowed his son to climb the aircraft steps by himself the following year as some forty cameramen snapped eagerly away to provide delightful pictures for a doting public. And the whole country was thrilled to see the young Prince standing, for the first time, on the balcony of Buckingham Palace after the Queen's Birthday Parade just before his second birthday – especially when his cousins Peter and Zara Phillips suddenly delivered two simultaneous kisses on each cheek!

For the many people who have been disappointed not to see Prince William featured in the Queen's Christmas broadcasts, or puzzled by the fact that, unlike his cousin Peter Phillips, he has never been seen in the Queen's arms since his christening, the explanation must surely be, once again, that too much publicity, the risk of premature identification with the oppressive solemnity and paraphernalia of sovereignty, will be harmful to the kind of upbringing everyone in the family wants for the two Wales children. To date, Prince William's life has revolved around his parents' two homes; the somewhat restricted, even gloomy Kensington Palace apartments which also serve as the Prince and Princess' official London headquarters, and Highgrove, the spacious Georgian mansion which stands in some 350 acres of farmland in the heart of Gloucestershire. All the indications are that Prince Harry's life will follow a similar pattern. Because his parents like to be near, or at least within constant reach of their children, their weekday existence will be spent at Kensington Palace for some thirty weeks in the year, so that both parents can, unless on official visits to the provinces, combine their office work with the luxury of their children's company, and enjoy the opportunity to take a much more active part than all their predecessors in title in supervising their upbringing. But it is at Highrove that Prince Harry and his brother will benefit from the real cosiness of family life. Because of the wide open spaces of the estate, here is a degree of privacy which means that the royal pram, and later the pushchair, can be wheeled out as often as desired, without the constant need for nannies to look over their shoulders for pursuing pressmen. Here, too, the baby can enjoy as much fresh country air as any parents could wish for their children, without the too obvious presence of detectives, or the police alerts which even the briefest foray from Kensington Palace into the parks of London inevitably involve. And, thanks to recent developments initiated by Prince Charles, both his children will soon be able to venture out of doors to watch the Beaufort Hunt pass through the estate during the autumn and winter months, or to visit the parade of craft workshops set up on the edge of the Highgrove estate only this year as part of a Duchy of

Cornwall rural job creation scheme. Who knows what royal career might develop from hours spent watching chair restorers, woodcarvers, graphic designers and furniture makers at work?

Prince Harry will also be a regular visitor to all the traditional royal homes – from the grandeur of Buckingham Palace, Windsor Castle and Clarence House to the relatively initimate surroundings of Sandringham, Balmoral or Royal Lodge, Windsor. Such regular treats await all new royal recruits. But the royal visiting round will only be half the story. Prince William has been a frequent visitor, with his parents, to the Princess of Wales' family seat at Althorp in Northamptonshire – indeed he attended the 60th birthday celebrations of his grandfather, Earl Spencer, there in May 1984 – and the Princess will be eager to take her second child there as soon as possible. Although the 17th-century stately home is open to the public, there is a strictly private part of the house which only family, friends, special guests and those wealthy tourists who can afford anything up to £100 a head to dine with the Spencers, will ever have a chance to see. It includes a nursery which the Earl and Countess renovated especially for Prince William in 1982, as part of a massive £1 million refurbishing scheme (which included removing mushrooms and toadstools from some of the walls) paid for by the controversial sale in the last three years of over £2 million worth of art treasures, including paintings, furniture and silverware. In those private quarters, too, are the corridors where Princess Diana and her younger brother used to play hide and seek, the staircase down which they slid on tea trays, and a newly decorated Elizabethan Room which, says Earl Spencer, 'is wonderful for playing bears in.'

Althorp is only one of several properties now owned by Lord Spencer. He has country homes in Norfolk and Brighton, and a London flat, which serves as a useful *pied-à-terre*, in place of the now abandoned Spencer House. One of the last great aristocratic houses in London, Spencer House overlooks St James's Park, and has been owned by the family for three centuries. But for decades, because its upkeep as an occasional family base is prohibitively costly in current economic circumstances, it has been leased to various organisations, while attempts to sell it outright have consistently failed. So the young royals will perhaps not give it much of a thought as they pass it on their way to the Spencers' most recently acquired property on the south coast. These are the three Spanish-styled seaside houses near Bognor, which Lord Spencer has purchased within the last two years, and where the growing Wales children may in future years be spending a few days of their summer holidays before flying north to Balmoral to join the Queen.

The most likely candidate for these visits is the principal house, Tradewinds, which was bought, along with a smaller adjacent property called Hacienda, in September 1982 for around £½ million realised out of Lord Spencer's private investments. They stand in two acres in what is now acknowledged as an exclusive upper-crust estate at Aldwick Bay, and Tradewinds, with its patios, cloistered terraces, and the matador weather-vane on its squat tower, boasts five bedrooms, as many bathrooms, four reception rooms, a garden room, a sun room, a study and a gun room. It also has its own private swimming pool and a sauna, and affords garaging for up to six cars. Both front and back gardens have rockeries and are beautifully lawned, the front being screened from a private drive by trees and hedges, the rear also flanked by trees on both sides as it runs down to the private shingle beach. Just along the coast stands Lord Spencer's third retreat, Water's Edge, purchased at the beginning of 1984 for £160,000. Like the others, it is a detached house, though much smaller than Tradewinds, offering only four bedrooms and a two-car garage, and painted cream as opposed to the dull red of the Aldwick properties. But it lacks nothing in style, with its huge concrete lions guarding the main gates and a superb dolphin fountain in the grounds. And it is within a stone's throw of Craigweil House, where King George V spent almost fourteen weeks recovering from severe septicaemia in 1929.

Whether on holiday or not, Prince Harry will certainly not lack for playmates. Kensington Palace itself will offer an almost bewildering choice, with three-year-old Lady Gabriella Windsor, daughter of Prince and Princess Michael, on one side, and Lady Rose Windsor, the four-year-old daughter of the Duke and Duchess of Gloucester, on the other. And at the bottom end of the long driveway that separates the palace from Kensington High Street are grace-and-favour quarters where four-year-old Laura and 18-month-old Alexander Fellowes will welcome their latest cousin. They are the children of the

Princess of Wales' sister Jane and her husband Robert, a stockbroker by profession who is now the Queen's assistant Private Secretary – hence the residence within the grounds of Kensington Palace. Even closer in age to the new baby is another cousin on the Princess' side – Emily, the fifteen-month-old daughter of Diana's eldest sister, Lady Sarah McCorquodale, but the chances of Emily and Prince Harry seeing much of each other are comparatively slim, as Lady Sarah lives up in Lincolnshire, where her husband farms.

Highgrove will offer no shortage of opportunities for Prince Harry to see other cousins. Not only will Prince and Princess Michael of Kent and their young family be just a few miles away at their country home at Nether Lyppiatt, but those two mischievous Phillips cousins, the children of Princess Anne, will be on hand at nearby Gatcombe. In addition, the Prince and Princess of Wales will soon be introducing Prince Harry to some of their closest friends, most of whom are distant relatives. First and foremost will come the Romseys, at whose Hampshire home, Broadlands, the Prince and Princess spent the first three days of their honeymoon. The late Lord Mountbatten's senior grandson, and heir to the title after his mother Countess Mountbatten, Lord Romsey has two children by his attractive wife, Penelope – a three-year-old son, Nicholas, and a year-old daughter, Alexandra. You can't help concluding that their names were chosen to reflect the good memories Lord Mountbatten had of his doomed uncle and aunt, Nicholas II, the last Tsar of Russia, and his Empress, Alexandra – a consideration which would certainly have endeared both children and parents to Prince Charles, who has never made any secret of his own 'overdeveloped sense of history.' It is therefore unthinkable that the Wales and Romsey youngsters will not be encouraged to maintain the Mountbatten-Windsor ties which have existed for a century and a quarter.

Close on the heels of the Romseys are the Westminsters. The present duke, barely thirty years of age, is the wealthiest man in the country, owning a sizeable chunk of the most prestigious part of Mayfair and the West End, and rejoicing in what must be the most sought-after status symbol of all – that of being landlord to the Americans, who lease their London embassy from him. His wife Natalia is a great-granddaughter of the Grand Duke Michael of Russia (a cousin of Mountbatten's uncle, Nicholas II) and the couple have two daughters, Tamara, aged four, and Edwina, aged three. Both will no doubt be taking a maternal interest in Prince Harry, as will Lady Eloise Anson, the two-year-old daughter of the Earl and Countess of Lichfield. Lord Lichfield, related to Prince Charles through the Queen Mother's family, was responsible for those superb wedding day photographs of the Prince and Princess of Wales, perhaps the most celebrated of all his many royal assignments in the last fifteen years. His wife, by whom he also has two elder children – Thomas, aged five, and Rose, aged seven, is the sister of the Duke of Westminster. Another of his sisters married the Duke of Roxburgh, and their ten-month-old son, Lord Edward Innes-Ker, is sure to be another of Prince Harry's close friends. When Lord Edward was christened in April 1984, Prince Andrew was one of his godparents, and Princess Margaret has also been a regular guest at the Roxburghs' country seat, Floors Castle near Kelso.

Despite the informality of his name, Prince Harry will thus be raised within a fairly tight social circle, and it is almost inevitable that, however busy his parents' public lives are, his earlier years will be most strongly influenced by his immediate family surroundings. Comparisons with Prince William's upbringing are bound to be made, and people are certain to ask whether the younger child will not eventually suffer from the public attention given constantly to the elder, just as the elder might initially develop a jealousy towards the new arrival. Princess Margaret has often denied that she felt any sense of injustice at the prospect of her elder sister being groomed for kingship, though Princess Anne has occasionally hinted that she was frequently put out by the attention which the public gave to the young Prince Charles, rather than to her. Prince Andrew certainly does not seem to have lost out by being the second son. He has grown up to be an outgoing, confident young man whereas Charles was, if anything, much more introspective and contemplative. Indeed, no-one can be more aware of the pitfalls of a royal upbringing than Prince Charles himself, while no-one is more anxious to achieve a balanced childhood for both Prince William and Prince Harry than their mother. Both parents realise that their own childhoods were not totally happy experiences. Diana came from a broken home; Prince Charles from one where family life

was one of constant disruption in those very early, formative years when his parents were frequently abroad, deputising for the ailing King George VI. Thus far, the Prince and Princess have been able to give Prince William a sound start to life, satisfying public demand with good grace, taking him abroad with them where possible, yet by avoiding the danger of exposing him to unhealthy public curiosity, retarding the psychological effects of his position in life until the last moment. It is for this reason above all that there is no likelihood of the Queen's abdication in the foreseeable future. It is doubtful whether she has any personal wish to do so in any event, but since she herself was only ten when she became, quite unexpectedly, heir to the throne, and since Prince Charles was barely three at the time of her own accession in 1952, she will wish to delay at least until Prince William's coming of age, the time when life for both him and Prince Harry moves inexorably into the higher gear.

Ultimately, questions about Prince Harry's education will have to be resolved. Like Prince William, he is almost certain to be a beneficiary of the more liberal attitudes towards royal education which the last two decades have witnessed. The Queen and Prince Philip inaugurated a bold experiment in the 1950s, when they sent Prince Charles first to Hill House School in Knightsbridge, then to Cheam School in Hampshire, and finally to Gordonstoun, the remote retreat in Morayshire which celebrated its 50th anniversary in the month of Prince Harry's birth. Prince Charles experienced some unenviable social problems at Cheam, being with boys who reacted injudiciously to the presence among them of a Prince of the blood royal, and we now know from Prince Edward that this elder brother did not enjoy his time at Gordonstoun, and that he talks very little of it nowadays. As it happened, he benefited enormously from his Gordonstoun schooldays, and few will deny that, as a result, we now have in him one of the very best – the most caring, sympathetic, hard-working and amusing – of all 21 Princes of Wales. But the educational experiment launched by his parents could have gone disastrously wrong, and left him something of a introvert – even a social wreck. He of all people will be eager to ensure that, whatever educational opportunities become available to both Prince William and Prince Harry in the next decade or so, he and his wife will select according to each son's character and abilities, and not blindly follow the practices of the past.

Because of Princess Diana's two-year patronage of the Pre-School Playgroups Association, one possible major departure, given a good public airing only shortly before Prince Harry was born, presupposed that he would go to nursery school, instead of being brought up by a governess until he was ready for prep school. The establishment tipped as the most likely royal choice was Pooh Corner, a nursery school not very far from Kensington Palace, which caters for children aged between 2½ and 5. Run by Mrs. Louise Ahrenbeck, who has firmly refused to say whether the Prince and Princess of Wales have ever approached her on the subject, it operates the Montessori system of pre-school upbringing, which aims to develop all five senses together, but only at the pace set by the child itself; to instill the concept of self-regulation rather than imposed discipline; and to intrude as little as possible into the child's own formative experiences. In theory, it is a novel and fascinating system; in practice it seems most attractive to Princess Diana because it was adopted by the Young England Kindergarten, where she taught for 18 months before her engagement, and because her own niece, Laura Fellowes, is already a pupil there.

Nothing serves to remind us of the relentless march of time more strongly than the thought that Prince Harry will not come of age until two years of the next century have elapsed. The fact also reminds us that, if the changes of the last two decades are anything to go by, the sort of career he will follow may be quite different from that anticipated for, say, Prince Andrew. As the second son of the monarch-to-be, it seems unlikely that Harry will escape a spell in the armed forces – a fate that has befallen all three of the Queen's sons, and which Prince Andrew himself has extended to a 12-year commission in the Royal Navy. Of course, the new Prince will in time be called upon to fulfil his share of royal engagements, just like Prince Andrew today, and to represent his grandmother – or eventually his father – abroad. But there are also indications which suggest that all this may not be entirely exclusive, and that, should he wish to pursue his own career – in commerce, industry, the arts or even sport – he may well enjoy the opportunity to do so. Princess Anne is the most obvious example of a member of the senior branch of the Royal Family to have combined, very successfully, the demands of her position with a series of supreme achievements as a competitive horsewoman, and there are signs that Prince Andrew

will be matching his growing list of royal duties with his budding ambition to become a professional photographer. His first major commissions, a portfolio for the 1985 Ilford calendar, and a photographic book scheduled for early 1986, were both clinched only recently. The Duke of Gloucester was all set to take up a commercial career as an architect until, owing to the successive deaths within two traumatic years of his brother and father, he succeeded not only to the Dukedom, but also to the business of managing the three farms run by the Gloucester family. Both the Duke of Kent and his younger brother Prince Michael have interests in the world of industry; both, like their brother-in-law Mr. Angus Ogilvy, combine their commercial directorships with the inescapable round of royal engagements.

For the younger generation of the Royal Family, finding jobs has been more of a necessity than a diversion, since few of them will ever be called upon to perform royal duties. Viscount Linley, the son of Princess Margaret and Lord Snowdon, has already established himself as a designer and craftsman in wood, while his sister, Lady Sarah Armstrong-Jones, has tried her hand at several other creative pursuits, including theatrical and graphic design, techniques of stained glass, and film production. She is currently working on the production of the film *A Passage To India*. Lady Helen Windsor, the only daughter of the Duke and Duchess of Kent, spent most of her time since leaving school as a receptionist at a Mayfair art gallery, hoping ultimately to secure a full-time and permanent job in the art world. With her uncle, Angus Ogilvy, as a director of Sotheby's, that might not be too long in coming. In the meantime, she has gone to Paris to complete her knowledge of French – and, no doubt, of *the* French – while her brother, the Earl of St Andrew's, has made good use of his university vacations to undertake charity work in India. Their Ogilvy cousins are similarly busy. James has already helped to edit four editions of a 'freebie' London magazine called *Freeway*, while his sister Marina has just crowned her school career with the achievement of being selected to undertake

the adventurous Operation Drake expedition in 1985. All in all, attitudes to royalty involving itself in careers and 'extramural' pursuits have certainly changed since the Queen came to the throne, and the odds are that, given the natural inclination, a sense of ambition, and the means of occasional escape from the royal round, Prince Harry will be able to operate a career in tandem with his inevitable royal duties.

The possibility is not without support from the astrologers. Like the Duke of Gloucester, Captain Mark Phillips and Angus Ogilvy, Prince Harry was born under Virgo, a sign which is said to bestow all the qualities he will need for carving out a career for himself. Among these are a strong sense of independence, a forceful desire for an active life, a shrewd, even hard-headed business sense, and an acute awareness of all attempts to deceive him. But he will also enjoy those gifts that will make him a useful, competent and popular member of the Royal Family – dependability, a sympathetic nature, kindness, a conscientious loyalty that puts country and family before self, and a public image of substantial tact and dignity. Add a touch of intuition, a lively, if somewhat dry sense of humour, and a physical attractiveness which, they claim, will involve him in two particularly deep emotional relationships, and you have all the makings of a well-rounded, pleasant and interesting character. That is no great surprise. It is, when you come to think about it, the invariable, suspiciously unctuous result of star-gazing in the wake of royal births. Whether we shall remember these confident prognostications when Prince Harry's adult character begins to emerge in the brave new world of the 21st century is arguable. For the moment, it is probably sufficient to know that, according to one astrologer, he will at least be well-behaved – "certainly much better than Prince William". His parents, who seem to have spent much of their time recently recounting horror stories of William's behaviour as it progresses from the mischievous to the potentially destructive, will be glad of that. We shall see!

BUCKINGHAM PALACE

Her Royal Highness The Princess of Wales was safely delivered of a son at 4·20 PM today.

Her Royal Highness and her child are both well.

Signed

15th September 1984